hair
trix
for COOL CHIX

hair trix

for COOL CHIX

the real girl's guide
to great hair

Leanne Warrick

Watson-Guptill Publications/New York

First published in the United States in 2004 by
Watson-Guptill Publications,
a division of VNU Business Media, Inc.
770 Broadway, New York, NY 10003
www.watsonguptill.com

PRODUCED BY Breslich & Foss Ltd, London
DESIGNED BY Roger Daniels

Copyright © 2004 Breslich & Foss Ltd
Illustrations by Debbie Boon
Text by Leanne Warrick
Photos pages 80–95 by Shona Wood

Special thanks to the cool chix in Watson-Guptill's teen focus group
for their ideas, feedback, and enthusiasm.

Library of Congress Control Number: 2003022803

Printed and bound in Hong Kong

ISBN 0-8230-2179-3

1 2 3 4 5 6 7 8 / 11 10 09 08 07 06 05 04

Contents

Get to know your HAIR

You may have spent a lot of time together, but isn't it time you said "hey!" to your hair? The better you understand it and know what makes it happy, the more fabulous it will look. We are all different from each other, and the same goes for our hair. The conditioner that makes your hair super-shiny, might leave your friend's hair limp and greasy. What you need is a haircare routine that's custom-built for you. Turn to page 8 and take the quiz to find out which type of hair you have, then flip to your very own Gorgeous Hair Guide. There you'll discover what it takes to get your hair looking amazing every single day.

What's Your Hair Type?

Do you know what type of hair you have? Take this short quiz, keeping track of your answers. When you're done, tally up your score and check out which Gorgeous Hair Guide is for you!

1. How long does it take after you shampoo for your roots to start looking greasy?
- A) Less than a day.
- B) It never looks greasy.
- C) 2 days.
- D) 1 day.
- E) 3 or more days.

2. Take a look in the mirror. Which of these statements best describes your hair?
- A) Thin, with a habit of looking limp.
- B) Wavy with dry ends.
- C) Shiny and smooth all the way from the roots to the tips.
- D) Flat at the roots but frizzy at the ends.
- E) Very curly or very frizzy.

3. What is your biggest pet peeve when it comes to your hair?
- A) It always looks flat.
- B) Split ends.
- C) You don't have one.
- D) The ends are dry, but the roots are always oily.
- E) It's so curly and big!

4. Take a single hair and run it between your index finger and your thumb. How does it feel?
- A) Slightly greasy.
- B) Squeaky because it's dry.
- C) Smooth all the way down.
- D) Smooth at the top but then dry toward the ends.
- E) Really crinkly.

Your score:

Mostly As: Turn to page 10 for Gorgeous Hair Guide 1.

Mostly Bs: Turn to page 12 for Gorgeous Hair Guide 2.

Mostly Cs: Turn to page 14 for Gorgeous Hair Guide 3.

Mostly Ds: Turn to page 16 for Gorgeous Hair Guide 4.

Mostly Es: Turn to page 18 for Gorgeous Hair Guide 5

Oily Hair

The oiliness is caused by your scalp producing too much *sebum*, the oil that your hair needs to stay healthy. Keep your hair mega-clean, though, and you'll have a shiny mane to be proud of.

SCRUB UP

Choose a shampoo designed especially for oily hair. This will dissolve the extra oil and let the real beauty of your hair shine through. You should wash your hair every day.

HAIR FOOD

Use a really light conditioner. This will give shine without weighing your hair down with even more grease. Concentrate the conditioner on the ends of your hair—the roots are already taken care of!

Lemon Rinse

MAKE YOUR OWN
Heavenly
HAIR
TREAT

If you have blonde, strawberry blonde, or light brown hair, lemon juice will not only help remove oil from your hair but will give you extra highlights into the bargain! Use this rinse on hair that is washed but still wet.

You will need:

- the juice from 2 medium-sized lemons
- sieve
- large bowl
- 4 cups (1.2 liters) warm water
- old towel

1. Pour the lemon juice through a sieve into a large bowl.

2. Measure 4 cups of warm water from the faucet, and pour it into the bowl.

3. Wash and condition your hair as usual, then lean over the sink or tub and pour the rinse over your hair. Wrap a towel around your hair and relax for ten minutes before drying your hair as usual.

Dry Hair

What your hair needs is a little **T.L.C.** Nourish it and care for it, and it will reward you by being bouncy and shiny.

SCRUB UP

Don't wash your hair more than you have to. Your hair needs to hold onto its natural oils, and over-washing will strip these away. Shampoo when you need to, but no more than every other day.

HAIR FOOD

Use a thick, rich conditioner. This will moisturize your hair and replace missing oils.

Banana-and-Honey Hair Mask

MAKE YOUR OWN
Heavenly
HAIR
TREAT

This mixture of bananas and honey packs a real punch of moisture—plus, it will leave your hair smelling divine!

You will need:

- 1 ripe banana
- 2 teaspoons honey
- large bowl
- wooden spoon
- plastic wrap
- old towel

1. Squish up the banana in the bowl. Add the honey and stir well.

2. Shampoo as usual, then smooth the gooey mixture onto your damp hair. Wrap your hair in plastic wrap. Wrap a towel around the plastic wrap to trap in heat and help the hair mask to work.

3. Relax for ten minutes, then rinse your hair well and dry as usual.

Normal Hair

Lucky you! Haircare for you should be all about protecting what nature gave you—kind of like hair insurance.

SCRUB UP

Wash your locks every *other* day with a shampoo designed for normal hair. There are plenty of great ones to choose from!

HAIR FOOD

You have the only hair type that may not need a conditioner. However, you can always add shine to your near-perfect locks with a medium conditioner. Look for one with an S.P.F. (Sun Protection Factor) of 15 to prevent the sun from fading your color and dulling that beautiful shine.

14

Magic Mayo Pack

MAKE YOUR OWN Heavenly HAIR TREAT

Max out your natural shine with this strange-sounding hair treatment. Weird as it might feel, this pack will not only add shine, but also temporarily mend split ends, too.

You will need:

- 2 tablespoons mayonnaise
- plastic wrap
- old towel

1. Smooth the mayo through damp hair after shampooing, then wrap your hair in plastic wrap. Wrap a towel around the plastic wrap to help the hair mask to work.

2. Relax for ten minutes, then rinse your hair well and dry as usual.

Combination Hair

Your hair suffers from a split personality. It's too oily to be called dry, but those ends are frizzing out big-time.

SCRUB UP

Use a shampoo for oily hair, but massage it only into the roots. Don't worry about the ends as the shampoo will run down and clean them when you rinse.

HAIR FOOD

What's important for you is where you put the product. It's the ends of your hair that need conditioning, so do the opposite of what you did while shampooing and use your conditioner only on the ends—keep it away from those roots! Choose a conditioner for dry hair, and leave it on for a minute before rinsing.

Lavender Rinse

MAKE YOUR OWN Heavenly HAIR TREAT

Lavender is great for oily roots because it helps dry them out, but it's still gentle enough not to stress out those dry ends. The scent will make you feel pretty blissed-out, too! Lavender essential oil is easy to find at drugstores and health-food stores.

You will need:
- 3 drops lavender essential oil
- 1 cup (250 ml) warm water
- small bowl

1. Make a soothing tonic for your confused hair by adding lavender essential oil to a bowl of warm—not hot—water.

2. Shampoo and condition as usual, then rinse the mixture through your hair. Dry your hair as usual.

Very Curly or Frizzy Hair

Your hair is really porous, which means that it absorbs moisture like a sponge! Treat it gently and keep it moisturized to guarantee a healthy, luscious shine.

SCRUB UP

This type of hair can be tricky to shampoo, as it's very dense. Try rubbing shampoo onto dry hair, making sure it's spread evenly across your head. This is easier than applying shampoo to wet hair. Make sure you rinse your hair well after shampooing.

HAIR FOOD

Look for conditioners that contain *keratin*, which will deliver a hefty dose of moisture to help smooth the surface of your hair. If you can't find a conditioner containing keratin, choose one for very dry hair. Towel dry your hair first so that more of the conditioner gets where it's needed.

Olive-Oil Slather

MAKE YOUR OWN
Heavenly
HAIR
TREAT

Give your thirsty hair a good drink with this hot oil treatment.

You will need:

- 3 tablespoons olive oil
- large bowl
- small bowl
- plastic wrap
- old towel

1. Fill the larger bowl halfway with hot water from the faucet. Pour the olive oil into the small bowl, then set that into the water-filled larger bowl. Leave to warm for ten minutes.

2. Smooth the warm oil through your dry hair. Wrap your hair in plastic wrap, then wrap a towel over the plastic wrap and relax for ten minutes. The warmth will open your hair's cuticles and let in the goodness—mmmm! Shampoo out, then dry your hair as usual.

Warning!

The oil in this mixture can leave the sink or tub slippery after you rinse your hair, so make sure you clean it carefully when you're done.

Hairology 101

With the zillions of hair products, tools, and appliances out there, a girl can get a little confused. When it comes to hair, knowledge is power, so why not brush up on your hairology?

PRODUCTS...
What does What?

You'll find it much easier to get your hair looking the way you want it to with a little help from the right gunk. But hey, don't get carried away—always go easy with the product. You can add more if you need to, but overload your "do" with goo and you'll just have to wash it out and start over.

Gel

Gel is used to keep a style in place. Use it on dry hair for a slicked-back style, or to make funky spikes on short hair. Once dry, gel holds a style until it's washed out. Depending on the type of gel, it can also be used to create a wet look.

Wax

Wax makes flyaway hairs stay where they're supposed to, and is perfect for defining sections of hair. Wax should be used only on dry—not wet—hair.

Rub a little wax between your palms, then use flat hands to smooth it through your hair. Use fingertips to define the tips. Keep wax away from the roots to avoid a greasy look.

Hair spray

Got your hair just how you want it? Hair spray freezes your style in place. Spray a mist over your whole head when you're happy with your look, making sure to keep your eyes closed. Choose a light hold that will hold your style in place gently without making it look like straw.

Serum

This frizz-fighter turns frazzled hair to silk in seconds. A tiny amount smoothed through long locks will calm big hair or give curls a boost. Use on dry—not sopping wet—hair.

Straightening balm

If you have curly or wavy hair, blow-drying it straight can be hard work. Straightening balms or gels help to relax the curls and kinks in your hair, smoothing and calming it into silkiness. Smooth a blob of balm through damp hair before drying.

Mousse

Mousse will give your hair lift and volume. Use a golfball-sized blob on medium-length hair, slightly less on short hair, and a couple of blobs on really long hair. Comb the mousse through towel-dried hair before blowing it dry. You'll find your hair will have much more bounce, and will keep its style longer.

Shine spray

This is a great product to give a finishing sheen to your style. Hold the can 6 inches (15 cm) from your hair and give it a couple of squirts. Note that girls with curly or frizzy hair should use shine spray sparingly.

Curl enhancer

Wake up curls and add bounce and definition to your ringlets with one of these clever spritzes. The best time to use this product is on damp hair, before you scrunch it dry.

TOOLS... which ones do I need?

Using the right tools for the job means you will be able to get the style you love easily and without damaging your hair.

Paddle brush
A paddle brush has a wide, flat back and is great for smoothing long hair. It kills annoying static and encourages shine.

Round brush
Round brushes come in different sizes and have different uses. Larger ones are great for blow-drying hair smooth or creating big, glamorous waves, while smaller sizes are handy for making tighter curls or flicks at the ends of your hair.

Vent brush
Use this when blow-drying your hair. The slots in the back of the brush let the hot air sneak through so your hair dries a lot faster.

Tail comb
This looks like a regular comb except that it has a long, pointed handle—like a tail. You can create a perfect part with one of these. Tail combs are also great for sectioning your hair when you're styling.

Wide-tooth comb
This is the only comb you should use on wet hair. Use one to spread conditioner through nice and evenly, and say bye-bye to tangles.

Fork comb
A fork comb, also called a pick, has only a few "teeth" and so is great for curly, wavy, or frizzy hair. Use one to separate out your curls without turning them to frizz.

APPLIANCES...
What does What?

All of these appliances get very hot, so handle them with care!

Hair dryer
This is more than just a speedy tool to dry hair! You can also use it make your hair straighter or curlier than usual. For straight hair, use clips to divide your hair into sections, then focus on one section at a time, pulling it taut over a round brush as you dry. To bring out your natural waves or curls, pile your hair into a diffuser attachment.

Flat iron
A flat iron will get your hair poker-straight for a super-glam look. When using a flat iron, protect your hair by coating it first with a leave-in conditioner. Straighten hair in sections, starting at the top and gliding the iron down to the ends, keeping the iron moving the whole time.

Crimper
These come with different attachments for various depths of crimp, from a gentle wave to really crinkly. Do your whole head or make "stripes" of crimped and straight hair.

Curling iron
Even the straightest-haired girls can have Rapunzel-like curls. Before using a curling iron, let it heat up for five minutes on a heatproof surface. When it's ready (usually there's a light that will click on or off to tell you), wrap small sections of hair around the iron and hold for just a few seconds to create a perfect ringlet. These will stay put better with a spritz of hair spray.

Hot brush
A hot brush is fabulous for curling or straightening towel-dried or dry hair. It's also great for perking up tired or flat hair when you don't have time to wash and restyle it. If you get the kind that's battery operated, you can just pop it in your purse and use it whenever you need a lift!

Get Salon Savvy!

Hair salons can be pretty scary places—
after all, your precious locks are at stake!
There are so many hairdressers and salons out
there, how do you find one that's right for you?
And how do you make sure you won't walk out
with a style that's totally different than what
you'd imagined?

Finding a salon

The best way to find a salon is to talk to
friends. Have they found a salon or stylist they
like? Ask them about the salon. Are the stylists
friendly and, most importantly, do they listen?
Write down the names of stylists that your
friends recommend, then call and see if you
can get a "consultation" (see page 28 for more
about consultations).

If you see someone in the street with hair
you love, don't be shy: Go ask her where she
got it styled. She will be thrilled and you'll get
a good lead!

Before you go

Have a clear idea of what you want. Look through magazines and rip out any styles you like. Now, lay them on the table and get real. Which ones would really work on your hair? How much time do you want to spend on your hair each day? Styles work best if they match the natural texture of your hair. If you're a curly girl, you're not going to get a sleek bob without a lot of styling, and do you really want to spend your life plugged into a flat iron? Best to weed out the unrealistic styles so that you're left with a couple of options to take with you to the salon.

A consultation

Once you've chosen a salon, call up and schedule a consultation. This is like a mini appointment before the real thing. Best of all, it's free, so you can get a feel for the place before committing any cash. The stylist will feel the texture of your hair and find out from you what kind of look you would like. You should now show your pictures, as this is way easier than trying to describe a style. The stylist will let you know if he or she thinks that your chosen style will work. Don't panic if they say no. With a little more chatting, you'll be able to find a look that you like and that your stylist can bring to life.

AT YOUR APPOINTMENT

Relax and enjoy! Your stylist knows what you want and can get on with the serious business of cutting. Still, always be aware of what's going on while your hair is being cut. If you feel uncomfortable at any time, never be afraid to speak up. A good stylist would prefer you to say what you think rather than staying quiet as a mouse until the end and then being unhappy with your cut. Watch carefully how your stylist dries and finishes your hair. Ask what products he or she is using and get some tips on how to get the same results at home. Don't be afraid to write stuff down if you think you might forget—you'll be glad you did!

TIME TO GO HOME

If you're happy with your hair, make sure you tell your stylist—the next time you visit, he or she will remember just how you like it done.

Hairstyles

On the following pages, you'll find hairstyles to fit any kind of mood or occasion. Looking for a casual look? Check out Everyday Styles on page 34. Want something with a little more flair? Turn to Hang-out Styles on page 48. Is glamour what you crave? Look no further than Special Styles on page 62. Each section contains ten great styles, so you're bound to find what you're looking for!

Hot Tip

Sad because your hair texture won't work with the style you want? Don't worry—that's what curling irons and hair dryers are for! Turn to pages 22–25 for tips on products and appliances that you can use to make your hair curlier or straighter than usual. To blow-dry your hair poker-straight, you can also check out Simply Chic, on page 59. Then turn back to the style you want and get started!

Hairstyle Symbols

These handy symbols will tell you which types of hair work best for each style. Take a minute to get familiar with them so you'll know which styles are right for you.

How long does your hair have to be for a style to work? These symbols will tell you:

And what about texture? Check 'em out:

 Hair that's chin length or shorter

 Hair that's between chin and shoulder length

Hair that's longer than shoulder length

Straight hair

 Wavy or slightly curly hair

Very curly or frizzy hair

Who Do You Want To Be Today?

How you style your hair should totally depend on how you feel and what you're doing. You might want a special look for a party or event (lucky you!), or something more casual for hanging out with friends at home.

To find the look that's perfect for you today, just take this easy quiz. When you're done, go back and add up your points to find your score. This will tell you which section of styles to flip to. There are ten styles to choose from in each section, so there's bound to be one you'll love!

1. Which of the following best describes what you're wearing today?
   A) Sweatpants and a snuggly sweatshirt.
   B) Jeans and a funky T-shirt.
   C) Your new, gorgeous, absolutely favorite skirt.

2. Where are you headed today?
   A) Just school, then you have a friend coming over later to hang out.
   B) You're off to the mall with the gang to do some serious shopping.
   C) Home. You have to get ready for the party of the year tonight!

3. Which of these styles describes how you'd like to look today?

    A) Cute and casual. Comfort is key, but you still want to look gorgeous!

    B) Chilled-out hippie. You're feeling pretty and natural.

    C) Moviestar glam. You feel like dressing up and glitz is where it's at!

4. Thirsty? What is your drink of choice for today?

    A) Hot chocolate with extra marshmallows. Yum!

    B) A mega-fruity smoothie. Healthy and delish!

    C) Something a little bubbly. Maybe seltzer and cranberry juice with lime.

5. What movie do you feel like watching?

    A) A Disney film. You need a dose of cute!

    B) An adventure flick. Action is what you crave!

    C) A Hollywood romance. Bring on the glamour!

Your score:

Give yourself 1 point for each A answer, 2 points for each B answer, and 3 points for each C answer.

5–8 points
You feel like kicking back and being yourself today. You want to feel comfortable, but that doesn't mean you don't want to look cool as well. Turn to Everyday Styles on page 34 and choose a style that will look great no matter what you're up to!

9–11 points
Feeling funky? You're ready to show off your unique sense of style with a "do" that will let your personality shine through. Turn to Hang-out Styles on page 48 for ten looks for a sassy sister like you. Go on, shake it up!

12–15 points
Roll out the red carpet! You are in the mood for glamour. You need a dazzling style that will be the perfect finishing touch. Whether it's promtime, a trip to the movies with someone special, or just a regular day that needs a little extra oomph, turn to Special Styles on page 62 for ten looks that will make you shine like a star!

EVERYDAY styles

These styles are for when you're just buzzing around doing normal stuff. They are all great for school, but you're also sure to find a style here that's perfect for dance class, swimming, or playing sports.

Sleek and Wild

The coolest thing about this style is the contrast between the super-sleek front section and the volume in the back. It's perfect when you don't have much time to style your hair.

SUITABLE FOR

Lengths   **Textures**

1. Smooth a blob of gel through wet hair, then use the end of a comb to section off a strip that is two inches (5 cm) wide.

2. Make a center part in the front strip and comb it down flat on either side with a fork comb. If you're having trouble getting it really flat, use bobby pins to hold the hair close to your head.

Hint

A pretty headband will help keep the front section of hair neat and smooth.

3. Scrunch up the back to encourage your natural curl. Or blow-dry it with a diffuser attachment to get even more volume.

35

Fat Braids

Making braids with thick or very curly hair will give you a cute, super-chunky look. This is a great style to choose if your hair is a little frizzy and out of control.

SUITABLE FOR

Lengths   Textures

1. Use the end of a comb to give yourself a center or side part that goes all the way down the back of your head, separating your hair into two sections.

2. Carefully divide each side into three sections. Begin braiding by crossing the left-hand section over the central strand, then crossing the right-hand section over the central strand.

3. Repeat until all of the hair is used up. Fasten each braid with a hair elastic that matches your hair color—the elastic will be practically invisible—or leave the ends loose for a softer look.

Perfect Pony

If you wear your hair in a ponytail every day, this is a super-easy way to give your favorite style a smart new twist.

S U I T A B L E   F O R

Lengths   Textures

1. Comb your hair back into a high ponytail. Fix the ponytail with an elastic, keeping a long strand of hair free underneath.

2. Wrap the strand of hair around the elastic three or four times, making sure the elastic is completely covered.

3. Tuck the end of the strand through the elastic, pulling it through so it ends up as part of the ponytail again. Comb the ponytail smooth.

X Marks the Spot

This style is great for short hair, especially when you don't have time to wash and style it from scratch.

SUITABLE FOR

Lengths   **Textures**

1. Warm a tiny dab of wax between the palms of your hands and smooth it through your hair to make it a little chunkier.

2. Use the end of a comb to divide your hair into three sections: the top and two sides.

3. Comb the top back and the sides down. Use two bobby pins in a crisscross shape to hold the hair back on either side of your face.

Twistin'

If you're growing out bangs, or if your hair just won't stay out of your eyes, then this is the style for you. It means you can wear your hair down, even when those bangs are driving you crazy!

SUITABLE FOR

Lengths   Textures

Hot Tip
If you have time, add a second twist on each side!

1. Brush your hair smooth (use a fork comb if you have curly hair). Give yourself a super-neat center part with the end of a comb.

2. Take a small section of hair from the front of each side of the part and gently twist.

3. Use an elastic to hold the two twists together at the back.

4. Choose two of your favorite barrettes to clip over the front of each twist. Cute!

Feelin' Loopy

Bored of ponytails and pigtails? This variation is just as easy, but has twice the funkiness factor. Looks amazing with bangs, but still cool without!

SUITABLE FOR

Lengths   Textures

1. Brush your hair smooth, then divide your hair into two low pigtails. Fix them with elastics.

2. Pull each pigtail through the elastic again, but don't pull your hair all the way through this time.

3. Use your fingers to make both loops the same size.

Hint

Twist the pigtails a little before you pull them through the second time. This will give the loops a neater look.

Gypsy Bun

Hippie chicks listen up! This style looks amazing with a long, flowing skirt or hipster jeans and a peasant blouse. It's the perfect style for lazy summer days.

SUITABLE FOR

Lengths   **Textures**

1. Gather the top section of your hair back into a ponytail and fix it with an elastic.

2. Twist the ponytail until it coils up naturally.

3. When this happens, wind the hair into a bun.

4. Secure the bun by sticking bobby pins through the end of the hair and into the center of the knot. Pull a few strands loose to soften the look.

Rope Braid

Regular braids are so over! Why go for the ordinary when this amazing new braid is so simple? If you're a straight-haired girl, do this on damp hair and you'll have beautiful waves the next day. Two styles for the price of one!

Hint

This style looks best on hair that is all the same length.

1. Comb your hair back into a low ponytail and fix it with an elastic. Now divide the ponytail into three even chunks and comb them so they are smooth.

2. Twist the right chunk of hair to the right. Next, cross it over the other two sections, then back beneath them to the right.

3. Do exactly the same with the center and left-hand sections.

4. Repeat steps 2 and 3 until you run out of hair! Secure the end of the braid with a pretty elastic.

45

Pretty Pigtails

This style is perfect when you want to get your hair out of the way, but still want something cooler than regular pigtails.

1. Use the end of a comb to give yourself a center part. Next, pull your hair into two regular pigtails, one at either side of the base of your neck. Fix them with elastics. Brush through the pigtails, using a fork comb if you have curly hair.

2. Add another elastic halfway down the first pigtail. Finish off with an elastic at the end of the pigtail.

3. Repeat for the second pigtail, making sure that the spaces between the elastics are the same on each side. (If your hair is really long, add more elastics, evenly spaced, to each pigtail.)

Hot Tip

Use elastics of the same color on each pigtail, or mix them up for a quirky look!

46

Neat Knots

This works well on hair that is longer than shoulder length. Wavy- and curly-haired chix should twist their pigtails extra tight before pinning.

SUITABLE FOR

Lengths   Textures

1. Use the end of a comb to give yourself a center part. Make pigtails on both sides of your head and secure them at the base of your neck with elastics.

2. Twist the first pigtail until it starts to coil up naturally. When this happens, tie your hair into a knot (like you would with string), with the pigtail as close to the elastic as possible.

3. Wind the rest of the pigtail around the knot and secure it by sticking bobby pins through the end of the hair and into the center of the knot. Add more pins to the knot until it feels secure. Make the second knot in the same way.

Hot Tip

Decorate the knots with brightly colored scrunchies, flowers, or mini rhinestone pins to turn them into something really special.

47

HANG-OUT styles

These hairstyles will help you look casual but cool. They'll look just as great worn on a shopping trip as they will to the movies, or even to a party. Your weekend style will never be the same!

Punky Plaits

This style is far quicker and easier than braiding your whole head, but just as cool.

1. Brush your hair to get rid of frizz (use a fork comb if you have curly hair), then use the end of a comb to give yourself a neat center part.

2. Scoop all but the bottom third of your hair into a high ponytail to get it out of the way.

3. Divide the loose hair into six sections, three on each side. Clip the sections to your head so they don't get mixed up.

4. Make a braid from each section, braiding as tightly as you can and stopping about 2 inches (5 cm) before the end. Secure the end of each braid with a small elastic, then add big, heavy clips that will weigh down the braids and look amazing!

5. Let the top section of your hair down and hold it away from your scalp to comb it smooth. The braids will peek out from under the loose hair.

Twists and Curls

Wow! This unique style combines the funkiest of twists with your natural curls.

SUITABLE FOR

Lengths   **Textures**

1. Comb your hair back from your hairline (use a fork comb if you have curly hair), then use a tail comb to section the front part of your hair into six even strips.

2. Working on one section at a time, twist the hair back from your hairline, picking up hair from either side of the twist as you go.

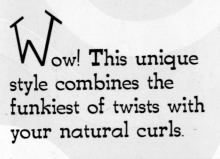

3. Secure the end of each twist with a small hair elastic, then pin each to your head using bobby pins through the elastics. Leave 2 inches (5 cm) of hair sticking out at the back.

4. Mist the back section with a little water, then blow it dry with a diffuser attachment (if you have one) to make it as curly as possible!

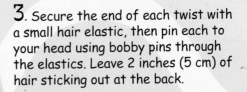

Accessorize!

Choose just one hair decoration? No way! Show off all your favorite barrettes and pins at once with this easy style, which looks extra special on straight, sleek hair.

SUITABLE FOR

Lengths   Textures

1. Before you begin, blow-dry your hair super-straight to get rid of any kinks. Do it in sections, pulling each section taut over a big round brush to get the very best results.

2. Use the end of a comb to give yourself a center or side part. Make sure the part is very straight and neat.

3. Now for the fun part! Take a selection of your favorite barrettes and pins and carefully slide them into position, starting at the top and working down your hair. Leave the other side of your hair sleek and loose for extra contrast.

51

Long Twists

This is a great way to get a funky look when you want to wear your hair down.

SUITABLE FOR

Lengths   Textures

1. Use the end of a comb to give yourself a center part, then brush your hair smooth.

2. Separate out three sections of hair on either side of your head, each 1 inch (2.5 cm) wide, and comb them so they are smooth and straight. Pin the sections down so they'll stay neat while you work.

Hot Tip

Customize your style by using a bright barrette to hold a twist or two back from your face.

3. Unpin the first section and divide it in two. Twist the first half on its own and secure the end with an elastic. Then twist the second half and secure the end of that one with an elastic, too.

4. Now twist the two halves together. Remove the two elastics and secure the bottom of the double-twist with a tiny rubber band. Repeat for each section right around your head.

Chunky Knots

Hint
Don't worry about getting the buns too tight. They should be as big and chunky as possible!

Curly hair can sometimes be hard to deal with. Banish the bad-hair-day blues with these cute, high buns. This is also a great style for girls with straight hair that's very thick.

SUITABLE FOR

Lengths   **Textures**

1. Pull your hair straight back off your face, then divide it into two high ponytails at either side of your head and fix them with elastics.

2. Braid the first ponytail, then coil the braid around the elastic.

3. Pin the braid into position with bobby pins. Braid and fix the second ponytail in the same way.

54

Funky Color

At last! Here's a way to experiment with color without having to dye your own precious locks. These streaks can be used over and over on all hair lengths. How did we ever live without them?

1. Choose some colored hair strands from a beauty supply store. Look for the kind with a comb clip fastening, not the messy kind you glue on. Hold the colored strands next to your own hair and carefully cut them to the right length.

2. Comb your hair smooth, then take the top third and tie it up into a high ponytail—this gets it out of the way for the important stuff.

3. Following the instructions on the pack, fasten the first colored strand as close to your scalp as possible, making sure you hear the "click" of the fastener before moving on to the next strand.

4. When you've attached as many strands as you want, let down the top section of your hair. Hold it away from your scalp to brush it smooth so you don't mess up the clips. Arrange your hair so the color peeks through.

Hair Wraps

Add color to your hair with one or more wraps. They should last at least three days, then it's time to choose a new color and start again. Wraps are tricky to do on your own, so why not ask a friend over and do each other's hair?

Lengths   Textures

1. You will need embroidery thread for this style, which is available at any crafts or sewing store. Pick out three colors and cut a strand 2 feet (61 cm) long of each.

2. Use the end of a tail comb to separate out a narrow strip of hair to be wrapped. (Choose hair near your face so it can be seen!) Tie the three strands of thread together and secure them to the top of the strip of hair with a firm knot.

3. Wind one of the colors around the knot to hide it, then continue winding the thread down the strip of hair. You will be wrapping it around the other two threads as well as the hair.

4. After you've wrapped a 2-inch (5-cm) section, pick one of the other threads to be the wrapper. Wind it tightly around and around the hair and the other two threads. Keep changing colors until you reach the bottom of the hair, then knot the threads as tightly as you can around the wrap. Trim off the ends carefully with scissors.

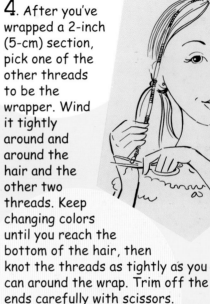

Hot Tip
The tighter you wind the wrap, the longer it will last!

Curl Power

Y̶ou'll need to use a curling iron to get this pretty half-curly, half-straight look.

Lengths   Textures

1. This style is very sleek and sophisticated, so start by using a hair dryer to get your hair poker-straight. Then use the end of a comb to give yourself a side part.

2. Use a curling iron to curl only the *middle* portion of your hair. To do this, take a section of hair, insert it into the curling iron, and slide the iron down to

about 4 inches (10 cm) from the end of the hair. Rotate the curling iron up until it is at the level of your eyes, keeping the ends of the hair straight. Repeat with the other sections until your entire head is done.

3. Spray a fine mist of hair spray over your lovely new ringlets to fix them in place without weighing them down with gunk.

Simply Chic

This super-sophisticated look is perfect when you want to keep the focus on your face and outfit—sleek, shiny hair is hard to beat!

SUITABLE FOR

Lengths

Textures

1. Wash and towel-dry your hair so that it is damp but not wet. Smooth a small blob of straightening balm through your hair with your hands, then comb it through with a wide-tooth comb to make sure the balm is evenly distributed.

2. Use clips to separate your hair into six sections, three around the top of your head and three around the bottom. (This is how hair stylists get blow-outs so perfect.) Wrap one of the bottom sections around a large, round brush, curling it under and pulling it taut. Blow it with your hair dryer until it is completely dry. Do the same for the other bottom sections, then the top ones.

3. When you've finished all six sections, brush through with a paddle brush and finish with a light mist of shine spray—wow!

Hint

Direct the air flow of the hair dryer down the hair. This keeps the look as shiny and sleek as possible.

Back Twist

Here's a new way to do half-up, half-down hair. This will work better and look neater if you have someone help you. And after all, isn't that what friends are for?

1. Brush your hair smooth, then gather up a small section from the top center of your head and twist it around to the right. Next, take a small section from the left side and bring it over the twisted section. Twist the two sections together a few times.

2. Take a small section from the right side and bring it *under* the twist, then twist the two together a few times.

3. Keep going, bringing small sections in from both sides and twisting them into the center twist. When your twist is long enough (this is up to you!), take a thin strand of untwisted hair from underneath the twist and wrap it around the bottom of the twist to make a band. Secure this thin band to the twist with a hair elastic.

Hint

This style will stay put longer if you do it on hair that hasn't been washed for a day or two. Your natural oils will give it extra staying power!

SPECIAL
styles

Want something a little more glamorous for a special event? If so, this is the section for you! These styles all have that extra "wow" factor that makes even the simplest outfit a stunner. Trust us, they are definitely worth the effort!

Girly Curls

Are you a straight-haired girl who longs for glamorous curls? Well, this is the style for you! If your hair is super-straight, comb styling mousse through towel-dried hair before using the curling iron.

Hint

Give your curls a longer life span by blasting them with the "cool" setting on your hair dryer.

SUITABLE FOR

Lengths

Textures

1. Use the end of a comb to give yourself a center part, then brush your hair smooth.

2. Loop strands of hair around one prong of the curling iron and then back around the other, making a figure eight shape. (Keep the iron away from your scalp.)

3. Put a cute barrette just below each ear to hold the curls back from your face.

Soft Side Bun

Add a touch of chic to your look with this simple and relaxed bun. Choose a hair decoration for your bun that matches your look—trendy? sporty? preppy? Whatever you want!

SUITABLE FOR
Lengths   Textures

1. Brush your hair until it's smooth and shiny (use a fork comb if you have curly hair).

2. Use the end of a comb to give yourself a side part, way over to one side of your head. Gather your hair into a ponytail behind your ear on the *opposite* side and fix with an elastic.

3. Twist the ponytail until it starts to coil up naturally, then wind it loosely into a bun.

4. Secure the hair by sticking bobby pins through the bun from all sides. Use a funky hair decoration around the bun to add your own personal touch.

Flirty Flicks

This sleek little style is a super-easy way to add a touch of class to short- and medium-length hair. It's also great for those days when you haven't had time to wash your hair. Ssshhh!

SUITABLE FOR

Lengths   Textures

1. Take a generous blob of gel and smooth it through your hair, using a wide-tooth comb to make sure it's spread evenly throughout.

2. Use the end of a comb or tail comb to give yourself a neat side part. Make sure the part is straight—this look is sharp!

3. Use a big round brush to blow-dry your hair super-straight, curling the ends out into flicks at the sides and the back.

4. When your hair is totally dry, fix the flicks with a mist of hair spray to make them last longer.

Twist Up

Here's an easy-to-do style that shows off hair with texture to its best. Love those curls!

Hint

Bobby pins come in different colors to match your hair—be sure to get the right color and they will be practically invisible.

SUITABLE FOR

Lengths   Textures

1. Divide your hair into three sections with the end of a comb. This will give you two parts, each going from front to back.

2. Twist each section once around and away from your face, then use bobby pins to secure the hair to your head. Leave the end half of each section loose.

3. Scrunch up the back to encourage your natural curl. You may want to blow-dry it with a diffuser attachment to get even more volume.

Flower Girl

Hot Tip
Complete your island style by smoothing away frizz with a little cocoa butter. A tiny dab smoothed onto each twist will add both shine and a lush tropical scent.

Aloha! Give your look a Hawaiian twist with this romantic, summery hairstyle. It's perfect for a beach party, barbecue, or even a luau!

SUITABLE FOR

Lengths   **Textures**

1. Brush your hair smooth (use a fork comb if you have curly hair), then use the end of a comb to give yourself a center part. Part each side in half again so you end up with four sections. Clip the sections in place so they'll stay neat while you work.

2. Unclip one section and gently twist the hair back, gathering hair from farther back as you go. When you reach the back of the top of your head, stop and secure the twist with a tiny elastic. Repeat for the other three sections.

3. Decorate your "do" with fresh flowers secured with bobby pins. The flowers won't last long, so leave them in water until the very last minute. Or cheat and use silk flowers—who's to know?

Sleek Side Part

Want to make short hair look really special? Easy! Here's a quick and simple look that's perfect for that last-minute dinner invitation.

Hot Tip

Accessorize with colored bobby pins or a glitzy barrette.

SUITABLE FOR

Lengths   Textures

1. Smooth a large blob of gel through your hair, using your fingers to make sure it's spread evenly throughout.

2. Use the end of a tail comb to give yourself a super-neat side part.

3. Tuck your hair behind your ears. Use the palms of your hands to get the sides flat and shiny by smoothing down hard. Blast with a hair dryer to set the style.

Glam Waves

You don't get much more glamorous than this! This style is easy to do on medium and long hair. You will need large **Velcro** rollers, which are available at drugstores and beauty supply stores.

1. Start with damp—not dripping wet—hair. Towel it dry after washing, then leave it to dry naturally for ten minutes.

2. Use a wide-tooth comb to get rid of tangles, then use the end of the comb to give yourself a side or center part. Section your hair into three strips—one down the back of your head and one down each side.

3. Split each section into three or four layers and wind each layer tightly around a roller. (The number of sections and layers you use depends on your hair: The thicker it is, the more you'll need.) Roll some of the curlers up and others under for a natural look. The rollers will grip the hair so there's no need for bobby pins.

4. When all of your hair is up, blast it with a hair dryer until you are sure it is completely dry. Carefully take out the rollers and use your fingers to separate out the waves.

5. Mist your hair with hair spray to hold the waves. But go easy—too much spray will kill your curls.

Spike Bun

Here's a cool new twist on the classic bun. Girls with extra-long hair might need to wind the ponytail around the knot a couple times to get the end short enough to spike up.

1. Brush your hair to get it really smooth, then pull it up into a high ponytail and secure it with an elastic.

Hot Tip

Decorate your spiky hairstyle with chopsticks. Just push one chopstick through the bun from one side and a second chopstick from the other, making an "X" shape.

2. Twist the ponytail so that it coils around onto itself. When the ponytail starts to look like a stiff rope, you know you've twisted enough. Carefully tie the "rope" into a knot (like you would with string). Try to get the knot as close to the elastic as possible. Leave the hair ends sprouting up through the center of the knot.

3. Secure the bun with plenty of bobby pins.

Ponytail Veil

This romantic style looks complicated, but it's really very simple to do. **The key is having hair that's all the same length**—it won't look as neat on layered hair.

SUITABLE FOR

Lengths   Textures

1. Brush your hair until it's really smooth. Sweep it back from your face, with no part. With the end of a comb, divide the front of your hair into three sections. Secure each section with an elastic.

2. Divide the center section in two, and pull each half over to join the left and the right sections. Tie these both off with elastics.

3. Bring the two sections together into one thick ponytail and secure with an elastic.

Élegant Up-do

Hot Tip

When you're done, mist a little glitter spray over the whole "do" for a fairytale sparkle!

Think fine hair can't be special? **Think again! This is the ultimate style for hair that lacks body.**

S U I T A B L E   F O R

Lengths   Textures

1. Brush your hair smooth, then gather it into a high ponytail and secure it with an elastic. If you want your look to be extra romantic, loosely twist some strands of hair before pulling it back.

2. Take a small section of hair from the ponytail and twist it until it begins to coil.

3. When this happens, loop it over and secure the loose end close to the elastic with a bobby pin. Repeat until all of the hair in the ponytail is looped and pinned in a loose heap on the top of your head.

4. Use your fingertips to mess up the loops a little, then pull a few strands loose at the front and sides of your head to soften the look.

HAiR
911

Everyone
has days when nothing goes
right hairwise. You know how it
is—when every glance in the mirror
brings a nasty shock? But don't think
that just because you're having a bad-
hair day you should pull on a
baseball cap and forget about it—
there are things you can do to save
the situation. For every hair horror
there's a magic solution!

OIL SLICK

Help! You've slept right through your alarm and now there's no time to wash your hair before you leave the house. What's worse, your hair looks limp and greasy. Try sprinkling talcum powder onto the roots and then carefully brushing it out. The powder will act like a thousand mini sponges, soaking up the excess oil. Another quick fix is to put your hair up in a ponytail and wash just your bangs, then blow them dry. Because this is the part of your hair that everyone sees first, this trick will refresh your whole style.

GREEN QUEEN

Swimming at the pool can be great, but afterward blonde hair can take on a greenish tinge. The problem is chlorine, a chemical used to keep the pool's water clean. Sadly, chlorine can also have a weird effect on light-colored hair. This is a really easy problem to solve. A hefty dose of tomato ketchup (about a cup) smoothed through damp hair will cancel out the green and restore your beautiful color. Leave in for ten minutes and then rinse thoroughly. Oh, and next time, use a bathing cap!

FLYAWAY FEAR

Fine-haired girls can suffer badly from flyaway hair, especially in the winter when the air is dry and hats are being pulled on and off. You might find your hair super-charged with a life all its own!

Next time your hair won't stay grounded, try this nifty trick. Grab a dryer sheet from the laundry room, and gently smooth it down over your locks. These sheets are designed to kill static in clothes and they'll do exactly the same for your hair. An added treat is the fresh smell they leave behind!

SPLIT PERSONALITY

If your hair seems frizzier than normal, take a close look at the very tips. You might find that you have split ends, which means that the ends of your hair have literally split into two. This is because the hair is damaged and dry. Fix this, and your whole head of hair will be revitalized, shiny, and beautiful.

Although you might not want to hear it, getting those ends snipped off is the only way to bring your hair back to its former glory. And although it can feel like it's taking forever to grow your hair, getting trims every six weeks will help the process along. Products that claim to fix split ends really just stick the hair back together temporarily.

DULLSVILLE

Sometimes it can seem like your hair is depressed, like it's lost its life and luster. What happened to the healthy shine you used to love?

Dull hair is often a sign that products have built up on the hair shaft. When there's too much residue on your hair, light has a harder time getting to it to reflect off of it. Thankfully, there's a simple rinse designed especially for this problem. Take 2 tablespoons of white vinegar and mix with 1 cup of warm water. After you shampoo, pour this over your head. Rinse immediately and condition as usual.

Make Your Own Hair Accessories

Now that you have all those fabulous new hairstyles to try, why not make some groovy decorations to finish them off? Drugstores are full of cheap, plain hair accessories just waiting for you to stamp them with your own unique style. Look around the mall for inspiration, then get crafty!

What's Your Unique Style?

Now that you have a healthy, shiny head of hair and a whole range of fabulous styles to pick from, it's time to whip up some cool hair accessories. Why buy the same old stuff at the mall when you can create something totally unique? Just take this easy quiz to find your personal style, then turn the page and get started. And while you're at it, why not make something for a friend, too?

1. Your closet is crammed to bursting with...
   A) Cargo pants and T-shirts—you like to look casual but stylish.
   B) Little dresses and cool skirts.
   C) Sweats of every type—they're so comfy!

2. When people meet you for the first time they are most impressed by...
   A) Your super-sophisticated style.
   B) Your down-to-earth attitude.
   C) Your amazing athletic abilities.

3. At school, which class is your favorite?
   A) Phys ed. You're happiest running round outside.
   B) Drama. It gives you a chance to show off your talent for performing.
   C) English. Writing poetry and stories is something you do for fun!

4. What is your idea of a perfect fantasy evening?
  A) Having dinner at an exclusive, fabulous restaurant with a gorgeous date.
  B) Watching a movie and gossiping with your best buds.
  C) Playing in a championship soccer game with your favorite teammates.

5. What do you usually wear to bed?
  A) A long nightie that's so pretty you could almost wear it to a prom!
  B) The warm, soft PJs that you've had forever. Who cares about the teddy design, they're so cozy!
  C) A big, soft T-shirt and pair of shorts.

6. The boy of your dreams is...
  A) A cute boy-next-door type who you could talk to easily.
  B) A drop-dead gorgeous guy with tons of style.
  C) The captain of the football team. He'd have to be super fit to keep up with you!

Your score:

Now it's time to add up your score:

1. A (1), B (3), C (2)
2. A (3), B (1), C (2)
3. A (2), B (3), C (1)
4. A (3), B (1), C (2)
5. A (3), B (1), C (2)
6. A (1), B (3), C (2)

6-10 points
Your style is classic and understated. You like accessories that won't go out of style in five minutes flat, and that you can wear with a ton of different outfits.

11-14 points
Your style is more about casual comfort than high glam. You adore bright colors and fun, sporty accessories.

15-18 points
You are addicted to glitz and love to stand out in a crowd. Your style is all about sparkle and glamour, with accessories that pack an extra punch.

Flower fancies

Want something pretty to decorate your ponytail or perfect bun? Head over to your local department or crafts store and check out their fabric flowers. Elastics, clips, and combs can all be given the flowery treatment. When you get bored with those flowers, just take them off and replace them with new ones!

FLORAL HAIR CLIP

This romantic hair clip will look great holding up your hair at a summer party or dance, and you can make it in seconds!

You will need:

- hair elastic with flower or other decoration
- plain hair clip

1. Okay, so this is cheating, but it's soooo easy and looks great! Just wrap the decorated elastic around the hair clip. Presto—instant flower clip!

DECORATED ELASTICS

Elastics come in so many colors, you're bound to find one that matches your outfit. Take a minute to add a few fabric flowers and you'll end up with a sweet, pretty hair decoration.

You will need:

• 10 mini fabric flowers on wire stems (found in the crafts store)

• 2 elastics

1. Choose little fabric flowers that match the color of the elastics. Bundle a few of the flowers together and twist the wire stems around the elastic to hold the flowers in place. Repeat for the other elastic.

Sparkles and glitter

Think you need to spend a fortune to decorate your hair with shimmery barrettes and bobby pins? **Think again!** These sparkly accessories cost next to nothing and are a cinch to make.

SEQUINED HAIR CLIPS

Stick-on sequins add razzle-dazzle to plain barrettes in the twinkling of an eye. We used silver and gold sequins here, but you can use whatever colors you like.

You will need:

- plain metal barrettes
- stick-on sequins

1. Peel the backing off the sequins and stick them onto the wide, flat end of each barrette. Easy!

GLITTERY BOBBY PINS

Hint
Protect your work surface with newspaper before sprinkling glitter over the bobby pins.

Gold nail polish and glitter are all you need to turn humble bobby pins into sparkly hair accents. Just remember to let the polish dry thoroughly before putting the pins in your hair!

You will need:

- silver bobby pins
- index card or piece of cardboard
- gold nail polish
- glitter

1. Put the bobby pins in a straight line down the edge of an index card or piece of cardboard.

2. Paint strips of gold nail polish across the bobby pins.

3. Sprinkle glitter over the wet polish and leave to dry.

4. When the polish has dried, tip up the card or cardboard and shake gently to get rid of any extra glitter.

Beaded beauties

In these projects, beads are sewn or glued onto plain accessories to turn them into beautiful, designer-looking hair decorations. Beads come in lots of shapes and sizes, so it's easy to find ones you like.

FUNKY FABRIC HEADBAND

Your local crafts store is the best place to find fabric trimmings and pearls for this one-of-a-kind headband.

1. Choose flower trimmings and beads to match the color of the headband. Arrange them on the headband as shown here.

2. Squeeze a dab of fabric glue onto the back of each flower and press it in place on the headband. Leave to dry overnight.

3. Sew the pearls to the headband in groups of three, as shown.

DIAMOND HEADBAND

This bejeweled headband will make you feel like a million dollars, but costs very little to make. Diamonds are a girl's best friend, after all!

You will need:

- stiff headband
- plastic diamonds with flat backs
- fabric glue
- stick-on crystals
- stick-on hearts

1. Squeeze a dab of glue onto the back of each diamond and press it in place on the headband. Leave to dry overnight.

2. Arrange the stick-on crystals and hearts around the diamonds, then get ready to party!

Hint

Arrange the diamonds and gems on the headband before gluing them down to make sure you like the way they look.

GLITTERY GEM HEADBAND

Glitter glue comes in all sorts of colors and is fabulously easy to use. Just squeeze it onto the headband and leave to dry. Here, we've used it to draw petal shapes around the diamonds and crystals.

You will need:

- stiff headband
- plastic diamonds with flat backs
- fabric glue
- stick-on crystals
- glitter glue in silver and green

1. Squeeze a dab of fabric glue onto the back of each diamond and press it in place on the headband. Leave to dry overnight.

2. Place the stick-on crystals on either side of the diamonds, as shown. Use the silver glitter glue to draw petal shapes around each diamond. Let dry.

3. Add more petals with the green glitter glue, then leave to dry overnight.

GLIMMER BARRETTE

This elegant barrette looks hard to make, but it's not. **The beads are simply strung onto a piece of strong thread and tied to the back. Want a change? Just add a different string of beads!**

1. Soft, flexible thread comes in a roll and is available at bead and crafts stores. Cut a piece of the thread that's twice as long as the barrette. Tie one end to the back of the barrette, keeping the other end loose.

2. String the beads onto the loose end of the thread. Stop when you have a string of beads as long as the barrette. Make a knot after the last bead to hold it in place.

3. Hold the line of beads against the barrette and tie the loose end to the back. Snip off any excess thread with your scissors.

Hot Tip

Many stores sell packets of beads in assorted sizes and colors, which is usually cheaper than buying them separately.

Cool Colors

If you thought paint was just for for walls, think again! Craft acrylic paint comes in every color you can think of and is easy to find in your local arts and crafts store. Pick up a few colors and a small paintbrush, then get busy!

If you're painting plastic hair accessories, it's best to sand them first with medium-grade sandpaper. This helps the paint "grip" the surface better.

CHIC CHOPSTICKS

It's super easy to pick up a pair of cheap plastic chopsticks and transform them into unique hair accessories. Paint the whole chopstick, or just the top. It's up to you!

Hot Tip

Use glitter nail polish to add some sparkle! Apply it in dots, stripes, or over an entire section.

You will need:

- two plastic chopsticks
- medium-grade sandpaper
- craft acrylic paint in assorted colors
- paintbrush
- paper towel

1. Wash and dry the chopsticks.

2. Rub the parts you want to paint with the sandpaper. Wipe off any dust.

3. Get your paints and paintbrush and go to town! Paint the designs shown here or come up with your own. Always allow each color to dry before applying the next, and be sure to rinse your brush thoroughly before changing colors. When you're done, stand the sticks upright in an old glass and leave to dry overnight.

index